# You're my favorite horse

### Richard H. Fox

ISBN: 978-1-945917-24-0

Printed in the United States of America

Cover design: Minnie Cho, FuseLoft LLC
Cover photo: Kristen LeClair

Also by Richard H. Fox:
*Time Bomb: Poems*
*wandering in puzzle boxes*
*The Complete Uncle Louie Poems*
*C is for Courage*, contributing author

"Making other books jealous since 2004"

Big Table Publishing Company
Boston, MA
www.bigtablepublishing.com

## Dedication

To Ann
the love of my life, my best friend, my pillar

To Dan & Bia, Adam & Jenn
the next generation, love you—it's your turn

To Mom & Dad
the Greatest Generation embraces mishegas

To Alan & Lynne, Renee & Marshall, Scott & Harriet
so blessed to be your little brother

# Acknowledgements

Grateful acknowledgment is made to the following publications in which these poems or previous versions first appeared or are forthcoming:

Alliance for the Arts: Broadsides Poetry Off the Shelf 2016—
    "Old Country remedies"
Alliance for the Arts: Broadsides Poetry Off the Shelf 2017—
    "An Assignation with Death"
*Boston Literary Magazine*: "Balance"
*The Broadkill Review*: "Quãng Ngãi Café", "Frog and toad are friends"
*Dual Coast Magazine*: "At sixteen on a balmy August day"
*Eunoia Review:* "Wallpaper peeling above the headboard"
The Gulf Coast Writers Association Poetry Contest:
    "Acceptance"—Second Prize
*Mulberry Fork Review*: "Uncle Louie and Simon Bell"
*OVS*: "How to tell my dog I'm dying, v. 1"
*Poetry Quarterly*: "An Assignation with Death"
*Radius*: "Frank Stanford sitting on a cumulonimbus near the gate that
    bypasses Purgatory"
*Sanibel-Captiva Islander*: "Memorial Day", "The new plot"
*Soul-Lit*: "How to tell my dog I'm dying", "The penultimate optimist",
    "St. Louis heat burst" as "You didn't say no"
*Strange Poetry*: "CANCER SUCKS! (yeah—I know that's 'trite,
    overused'. Bite me.)"
*The Worcester Review:* 'Skating on the edge of flesh", Winner of the
    2017 Frank O'Hara Prize

I have many people to thank:

John Hodgen—mentor, friend, teacher. Thank you for your patience and grace. You taught me how to find out who I am as poet and gave me the confidence to grow.

Janet Shainheit, David Thoreen, Cathie Spingler, Jennifer Freed—fellow members of John's workshop. I learn from your poems and your approaches to writing. Thank you for the opportunity to respond to your work, for your insightful feedback, for your friendship.

The writers in Sanibel Island Group #3 and the poets in the Tuesday Night group at the Alliance for the Arts in Fort Myers—thanks for giving me a home in SW Florida. Appreciate your diverse voices and senses of humor.

Nerissa Nields—for fine writing retreats, for introducing me to talented and inspiring writers, for your friendship, ADK-Northampton-St. Pete. I bring poems with vexing subjects to Big Yellow and they get written.

Jane Ellen Ibur—my sister-in-poetry, college classmate, companion seeker, Sestina whisperer, truth teller, bravest cowgirl, pockets filled with shells and similes.

Robin Stratton—friend and publisher, nurturer of new writers young and old, chaser of dreams fulfilled, literary light, beloved by community for kindness and support. Thanks for believing in me.

Jennifer Colella Martelli—appreciate your perspective and skill as an editor. You challenged me (what more could I want?) and elevated my poems while devising the ideal sequencing to tie their themes together. Much thanks.

The Hangover Hour at Nick's-Worcester—the funnest poetry venue in town. Thank you Dave McPherson for creating a home where words, performance, mayhem, and solemn hilarity blend into one smooth cocktail (have Sean pour a double.)

Worcester County Poetry Association—our community is diverse, healthy, riveting.

In Memory of Dan Lewis— generous, kind, graceful, courageous. A fertile poet without contradiction, Dan exuded presence: a body that accentuated, a voice that thrilled the room.

Carle Johnson—Dean of Worcester poetry. Thanks for your gracious welcome to all poets. You help us grow by offering wisdom and perspective. No one will ever shoot with a teddy bear better than you!

Anne Marie Lucci—a light, an angel, finest famous baker of hermits. Thank you for encouraging poets and giving spoken word a home.

Kristina England—how does one woman finish so many tasks with aplomb and finesse? Thanks for your friendship, advice, and kindness.

Sotirios Sam E. Lalos—you have a warm heart, a keen eye, and discerning ear. You are a valued friend and confidante.

Don White—hey buddy, thanks for laughing at my weak jokes. Your friendship and support is a true joy. Appreciate your willingness to join me in following a philosophical artery until it is tied off and begging for mercy.

Chloé McFeters—guide to those who seek healing, model of courage and determination. Your big heart leads us to renewal. Thank you for the opportunity to contribute to *C is for Courage*.

Jessica Jacobs—in appreciation of an invaluable manuscript consultation at the Sanibel Island Writers Conference 2016.

In memory of Marsha Kunin—my companion in art, literature, poetry, and the nature of existence. Thanks for laughter wrapped in pathos.

Thad Jones & Joe Chiuchiolo—any lies we tell are true. Thanks for 50+ years of friendship, adventure, and levity. Gee, we're old fogeys.

Clan Webster—It was real and is real.

# Table of Contents

## Divrei Torah

## Glossaries and Notes

# A Brave One

"The world is a mist. And then the world is
minute and vast and clear. The tide
is higher or lower. He couldn't tell you which."
~ Elizabeth Bishop


"And I circle ten thousand years long;
And I still don't know if I'm a falcon, a storm,
or an unfinished song."
~ Rainer Maria Rilke

## Balance

for Robert I. Haddad, M.D.

> "Life and death are one thread, the same line
> viewed from different sides." ~ Lao Tzu

### I.

My oncologist enters the exam room.
Doesn't freeze my nose or insert the hose.
He rolls on a stool to me. We sit
knee-to-knee. He whispers *I am worried.*

### II.

Sunrise, cramps, and caws wake me.
I stumble to the bathroom, void alone.
A crow asks *Are you afraid of dying?*
I answer *I am. I've never done it before.*

## how to tell my dog I'm dying

Bailey smells blood, discharge from my incisions.
He crawls on his belly, ears pulled back
when I groan, pillow to side, after a cough.

Bailey curls his back to my waist,
sniffs and stares in my face,
watches me spit into a bowl.

I need the toilet. He leaps off the bed,
trails me to the bathroom. I think back to
his puppy days, following him until he peed.

When I die, I want him to watch over me,
to know that my body became a corpse,
to know I didn't just leave him.

## The penultimate optimist

I don rose-colored lenses on red days.
My apparition trumpets words.
*Terminal terminal terminal,*
*Dead dead popsicle stick dead.*

I trace scars chest to side,
My funk flares, dawn's fog.
*Wake-feel, alive alive alive,*
*Pill pill docile savvy pill.*

I blare hearing aids on blue days.
My doctor poses chemotherapy.
*Palliative care, quality of life.*
*Faith faith grocery's grace faith.*

I romped our first radiation war.
My body marched, poisoned—burnt.
*White flag, sealed in casket,*
*Kill kill proportioned count kill.*

## Squamous Haiku: ICU dreamscape

First, do no harm. Last,
vacuum the queen's diary.
Unfettered spice.

Scattered climbing vines.
Rogue chameleon underfoot.
Whisper an ear lobe.

Nurse Eunice injects
heparin in my tummy.
Winks a keen smile.

My lips—fractured, numb.
Jalapeños hid amid
belly-button lint.

Redheads in blonde jokes
arrange ebony mirrors.
Mangoes meander.

Southern Cross contrails
rotate on transverse axes.
North Star moons Venus.

I'm alive today.
Defy my sure terminus,
I die by inches.

# The thoracic surgical pod: 4 a.m.

Nurse Jasmine opens the blinds,
hands me a container of pills,
styrofoam cup of water, straw.
She holds the water while I fumble capsules.
I get them down, stare at the walker—
four feet tall, three racks, two oxygen tanks.

She begins the five-minute routine,
transferring gear from wall to walker:
catheter, chest drain line, fentanyl button,
oxygen lines, oxygen monitor,
compression pillow. I examine my arms:
father's arms, thin,
purple-yellow blotches,
puncture patterns tracing veins,
skin flecked, Dead Sea.

She grabs me above the elbow on the tricep.
Counts one, two.
Pulls on two-and-a-half, my body sits.
The count again.
I stand, arms on the walker's
U-shaped padded dash—
oxygen to the left, bags to the right,
tissue box, water bottle in holders,
pillow, monitor in front bicycle basket.

We walk. I lean. Long halls.
One lap. Two laps. Three laps.
Jasmine coaches *in through nose,*
*out through mouth, purse your lips.*
Four laps. Five Laps. She squints sharply
at the monitor, boosts my oxygen flow.

I am stronger.

*One more lap.*

## The phlebotomist

sidles up to my bed,
blue scrubs with grinning dinosaurs.
I apologize in advance.
*Dad gave me lots of wonderful things,*

*but he also gave me his veins.*

She pokes my arms, pumps my fist.
We agree on a likely target.
*This needle's gonna burn.*
*No worries, I'm a cancer patient.*

I bid my body *go limp*. She digs in.

*Are you getting anything?*
*Got one tube full. Two more.*
I hear the second, third rack in her tray.
The interloper slides out my wrist,

She wraps my arm in blue tape.

*No green today? my favorite color!*
*Sorry, honey. Maybe tomorrow.*
*See you at 0500. Remember, pee by 0450.*
My compression pillow hugs my left side.

I cough—stabbed, spit out a strip, dead lung.

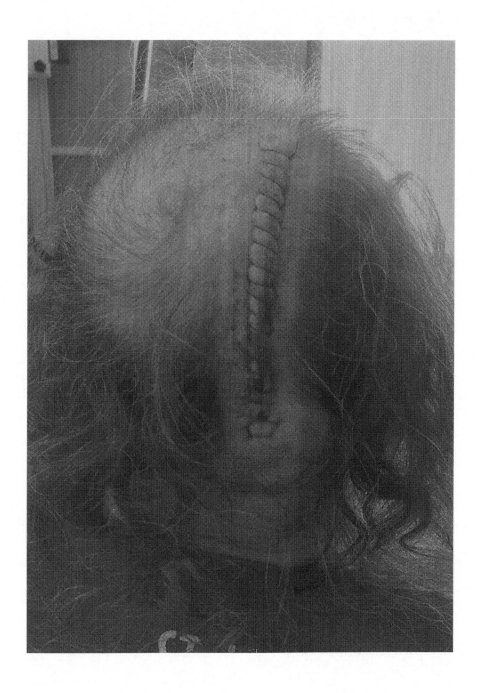

## Skating on the edge of flesh

One: on Dr. Paul Kalanithi's *When Breath Becomes Air*

The neurosurgeon.
     Cuts to cure.
     Midnight rounds/early call,
his wife waits for her consultation.

Ecstasy, saw slicing skull, a scalpel's rivulet.
Danger in the drill,
thrill in the skill.
     Sensitive hands, eyes that see
     what only he can see,
hope for goners.

Lung cancer killed the neurosurgeon.
     I have malignancies in my lungs.
     We share the trinity:
diagnosis, treatment, death.

He views the weight of a tumor on his new MRI,
     then its shadow, camouflaged, on the prior.
     His term: six-to-twelve months.
no time off for bad behavior.

The neurosurgeon parries death.
     I understand
          words carved into vellum,
          fingers swollen,
          steady.

Death is the ultimate deadline

I nod my head,
     tap feet to the beat of his verbs.
     Book and eyes closed,
     I see him wink,
     weep.

Two: Waltz of my neurosurgeons

Screened for a trial—
three options to fry cancer invading my lungs—
Boggle! A "nodule" appears in my brain.
Time to open my skull to new possibilities.

This neurosurgeon consults:
*I can't say you'll live longer with the surgery.*
*I can say you that without the surgery you'll die soon.*

It's all good, doc. Give it to me straight.
Clean lines don't cause pain.
Deadlines rearrange boundaries.

The neurosurgeons lead the mortality dance.
The guts to cut
to save to extend.
Young, sharp as titanium, repellers of storms.

Two days after surgery, 5:00 am, a couple of neuro-residents
bounce into my hospital room.
One taps my bandage,
peels top-to-bottom, length of the back of my skull,
snaps the stained white cloth, rolls it into a ball—
tosses a three-pointer
into the hazardous materials barrel
wedged open by the toe of his cohort.

5:00 pm, the curtain between me and my roommate divides.
The pair of neurosurgeons enter, arms extended, gentle nods.
They stand at the head of the bed, urge the fellows to emerge,
form two columns.

Residents, P.A.'s,
red-eyed interns, hunker at the bed's tail.

I have the most excellent rasta braid collar to crown,
flayed flesh, black stitches, greying hair.
A fellow points to his needlework.
The neurosurgeons exclaim *that boy can sew!*

One shows me the pre-and-post MRI's on his phone.
He beams *We got it all! The entire tumor!*
His feet slide-step.
He and partner grin,
tap fists.

They are magnificent,
masters of deadly sleight-of-hand.
I bathe in their love of dangerous duty,
absence of arrogance,
comfortable confidence,

my deadline extended.

## A Brave One

Here I am for you. Watch me smile, sit backbone parallel to couch cushions. Compression pillow hugs my left side, hides incisions, stitches, chest tube scars. Can't wear a shirt. The cloth sticks to sutures, scrapes scabs, adheres to the heart monitor glue. That glue? Circles all over my chest and sides. Sure, you can play connect-the-dots. We've tried mineral oil, alcohol, Purell. Next is Goo Gone. Not for skin but what the hell?

No, I'm not in much pain. Pop oxys. I won't mention downing MiraLax, stool softeners with each meal. Keep shitting tan worms. Mustn't block up the machinery. Yeah, eat three squares per day. But eating is work. Load every bite on to the fork, swallow, scoop up the next because the quicker done, the sooner the next oxy.

Sure, I'm a brave one. What else can I do instead of surgery? Let the cancer grow and die by inches? Courage is easy when it's the only choice. I beam. Walk an old man shuffle around the house for six minutes dragging my oxygen hose. Look how well I traverse the corridor over and over and over until the bell rings.

I chuckle, say I'm tired. Visitors stand, politely applaud. We all feel better.

It's simple to fake half an hour. To suppress the groans from a small movement of the shoulder. To cut off wails when I need to cough crap out of my lungs: phlegm, dried blood, bits of seaweed-green lung looking like spinach a sou chef sliced. It's ok. Spit in tissue. Tissue in bag. Bag in trash. Circle of healing.

It's simpler to mask the worst moments. Inhuman sounds from an unknown source. Fear, agony, despair not of body. My real enemy. Slam a foot into the car floor on the way home from the hospital, more tired than I ever knew I could be. The grating anger purses out my lips at my wife, the only person who hears me weak. I want to leap out the window onto this city street, crawl to the gray granite entryway, curl up on pavement, be rocked by underground trains.

## Noogies

Guess it's cool to make fun of a fogey,
        ponytail poking out a wide-brim hat,
        walking a brown mini poodle.

Yeah, you burn rubber, wreck tires,
        twerk fingers in the air at me,
        wave white rich boy hoodoo.


I had half a lung ripped out, have seven nodules
        on another lobe, could be surgical scars,
        could be more tumors.

Hey, tomorrow a new scan, see the surgeon,
        the oncologist, maybe start chemo—
        an expiration date on my ass.

## Categorical Shifts

Never a notice of pending resolution.
Never a choice from row A or B or C,
        a selection of side effects.

Ordinary ways to die from cancer:
        Pneumonia              Sepsis
        Metastases             Starvation
        Overdose              Suffocation


*Big Bang, Homeland*, Red Sox blur within TV.
Sage hallucinations blend commercials,
        sanitized lyrics from classic anthems.

Sing along! Free the wicked words:
        "All Right Now"           "Dream On"
        "Instant Karma"           "Time Of The Season"
        "We Should Be Together"   "Won't Get Fooled Again"


Color with mute crayons. Toss bread on a stream.
Family cleans up compounding troubles,
        faces frozen, voices cracking.

Justifications for surrender:
        Leaky diapers            Bed sores
        Dementia               Arthritis
        Anxiety disorders        Peace

## Acceptance

the otolaryngologist tolls
*You've got a tumor at the base of your tongue*
*—but you knew that*
*Take this paperwork to Tammi, she'll set up a biopsy*

              stag-
                     ger
       the                    hallway
              ceiling
       lights
                            disco-ball
       fireflies
              punctuate
              the walls

       clip the door frame with an elbow
    turn a corner into the reception room
drop forms on Tammi's desk

       smile (I think)

room shimmers clever gold      fetching mauve
       feel my body gone slack                faint
              wake to Tammi's waist asking *Are you okay?*

## Squamous Haiku: Malignant

Chemo waiting room.
Woman next to me blushes.
Dark chocolate kiss.

Lead-lined dungeon vault
camouflaged by children's art.
Where do we sign in?

Flayed monkey pose:
head lashed to metal platform,
hot blanket, knees wedged.

Post-radiation.
Random itches, roaming rash.
*S* on chest turns *8*

Scratches lace my skin.
Creams fail. Pills fail. Nails notch trails.
Obscure side effect.

Poem performed rote
disengaged after first verse.
My cut brain leaks words.

Malignant. Benign.
Wee range on a weigh station
between mute coils.

## CANCER SUCKS!
### (yeah—I know that's "trite, overused". Bite me.)
~ for Chloé McFeters

Cancer: To you,
      miracle debunks statistical improbability.

Cancer: You kill me, you kill you.
      Dude, are you suicidal?
      A microcellular terrorist?

Cancer: You stamped an expiration date on my ass.
      Why can't I read it in the mirror?

Cancer: You turn me into a chatty-Cathy
      when I have blood drawn or an EKG or a growth lanced.
      Clinicians have long days with doomed patients.
      I figure it's my job to provide laughter,
      pain not the priority rather the punch line.
      I want the applause of razors rending my skin.

Cancer: I shuffle in place, drool, adjust a face mask,
      rip off a dried bandage,
      fail to ace a flip to the corner trash can.

Cancer: I honor my quest.

Cancer: If I know I'm dying in days,
      should I order that cane from Amazon?

Cancer: You flapping freeloader,
      will you slay me from throat, lung, brain, or
      a random organ to be named later?

Cancer: Thanks for getting me cute lil' square steroids.
      Green is my favorite color.
      Three sleepless nights can be a drag but
      three manic runs of infomercials is a hoot.

Cancer: That expiration date?
   I appreciate knowing,
  being able to say what I want to say to the people I love,
  hear their words for me.
  Dying without warning would be crude, an
     untold
     undone
     mess splattered onto survivors.

Cancer: We live together—
    as beloveds? besiegers?
  You take food without asking,
     never clean up after your parties,
     leave diarrhea on the toilet seat.
  I had a flatmate like you in college.
     Him I got rid of with a month's rent check.

Cancer: I mean…
  what the fuck?

Cancer: Are we traveling together?
  Is dying younger an early admission?
    A kinder world,
      family,
      friends,
        my dogs?

Cancer: Are you an angel in disguise?
   Shredded nylon wings,
   makeup caked—stray
      vomit-piss-blood-shit?

Cancer: A topaz blade sparkles
     between azure teeth.
You balance a blinding beam in one hand,
    gesture with the other.

# On the nature of hope
~ for Jennie

she Stays Strong, arms bruised from needles
*food tastes like sour milk* she texts
pain sails across her abdomen, breasts
exploding hives—steroids add insomnia

       clinical trial radiation—body merely aches
       she savors a steak, potato, sundae
       walks the block waving to neighbors
       prays, faith in Jesus, faith in heaven

five months of remission, then
new twinge threatens her side
scans show traveling tumors
experimental chemo—side effect shingles

       she visits a niece for Christmas
       rocks babies, loves that family grows
       an amber star shines on her wedding band
       mistletoe tinsel, the ornament with her name

treatment shrinks to building dams
she emails me a photo, sunrise through heather
writes about weeding, planting bulbs, fertilizing
I send beach pictures—waves, pelicans, shell piles

       hospice—hospital bed, diapers, leg wraps
       her smartphone, battery dead, lies on dresser
       she vomits blood, black matter—indelible pain
       prays, faith in Jesus, faith in heaven

faith that her chrysanthemums will bloom

## In response to youthful Weltanschauung—redux
aka Reordering My Bucket List or Instructions For My Funeral

**original desires**                                                    **redux responses**


I want to be a smiling old coot,
fall asleep during phone calls.

                                                    No, a fogey typing
                                        prefaces, preambles, apologies
                                        while talking—maybe listening—
                                                    on the telephone.


I want to push a walker  s l o w l y
up the hallway, block young dudes
bouncing wall-to-wall looking
for a passing lane.

                                        My thoracic-designed lung-o-limo—
                                        dual oxygen tanks, U-shaped dash—
                                                    corridor right of way.


I want to drive 20 miles per hour
in a 40-miles-per-hour zone,
usher tailgating traffic.

                                                First month after surgery,
                                        my speedometer never passes 25 mph.
                                        I keep to back roads, school zones.


I want to park my car at a 15-degree
angle to the curb
like Dad and Grandpa.

                                        Really not an issue, really not a jam.
                                        Triangular curb-to-wheel-to-wheel shadow,
                                                    generous sign of my decline.


31

I want to lounge in a
four-way adjustable recliner,
seat rising to eject me when
standing is too daunting.

Still standing.
I do love my couch
and purple blanket.

I want to wear Coke-bottle glasses,
corneas blue whale eyes.

The TV,
hard to see,
confuses
bifocals
exponentially.

I want to have a pill box
with medication compartments for
wake-up, after breakfast,
before lunch, after lunch,
before dinner, after dinner,
bedtime.

Medications:
pills, capsules, soft caps, chew tabs—
round, square, triangular, pentagrams—
strawberry, cherry, vanilla, peppermint—
one chocolate-flavored chunk
more relaxing than Ex-Lax.

I want to wear a bib and
towel on my lap when I eat—
spooning, chewing, swallowing
tax powers of concentration.

The rule—
no white shirts at

32

Italian restaurants—
still enforced.
. Stain-Stick in every closet.
Feeding myself remains a gas.

I want to see my sons marry,
give me daughters-in-law to spoil.

I want my sons to live happy safe lives,
to love and be loved,
to never abandon their dreams,
to leave our world better than when they arrived,
to carry me always.

I want my grandchildren to chauffeur me—
I'll cluck at their music, chatter
about seeing the Grateful Dead play
Dark Star for 90 minutes one night in
St. Louis when I was 19.

This stanza must stay. It's important. It's me.
I need my grandchildren to know.
Maybe they'll download the soundboard.

Please play The Dead's "Box of Rain" as
people shuffle into shul (on schedule).
The Beatles' "Across the Universe" (off limits),
The Airplane's "The Other Side Of This Life" (with hope),
James McMurtry's "Cold Dog Soup" (for poets).

[I'd add The Beatles' "Tomorrow Never Knows"
but it's too edgy for a funeral.]

I want to celebrate
the second iron anniversary.

Holding out for ruby, sapphire, gold,
and emerald.

33

I want to watch the president
and her wife
congratulate
the first colonists on Mars.

For so many reasons.

I want to doze
in my boudoir's hospital bed—
intrigued by what lies ahead,
family reliving amusing stories
while I drift from this world.

Hearing is the last sense to go.

If I vigil,
chomp pizza, sip stout,
watch a ball game.
Release me.

I want to be met in the next
by family, friends—
my dogs welcoming me home.

# Lyrical withdrawal

"The great thing about getting older is that you don't lose
all the other ages you've been."
~ Madeleine L'Engle

"One day you finally knew what you had to do, and began."
~ Mary Oliver

**Frank Stanford sitting on a cumulonimbus near the gate that bypasses Purgatory**
"It wasn't a dream it was a flood." ~ Frank Stanford, poet (1948-1978)


I need a wingman to watch my back
lemme know when old Gabe turns his peepers my way
cat's ok when we mix chops with a bard beat
only horn player I ever met—
            no eye for the blonde in the front row


that poem I forgot I wrote turned into a hymn
            #1 with three bullets
                    Bach on harpsichord
            got myself this attic office
            quills, parchment, umber ink
a hymn a month, I stay golden


Old Scratch paces…waiting to collect
figures White Beard will see the real Frank
command Peter to dump me on down


but—maybe He sees what I never saw
                    collisions in my head
no peace until the poem's written        then
            moments before lyrical withdrawal
            —wild turkey run cold
bad poetry ruins good nights


never read aloud to a crowd
never taught my ver-sed tricks
coffeehouses and classrooms
buffets of sweet yearning smiles


call me prolific
I had no choice


some say I killed myself on account of my wife and mistress


you be the judge

## Taxi Dancer take two (May 1976)

At the wedding, she nudged me to dance.
*Give an old broad a chance* and I did:
fast, slow, slower.
But dance was an obvious metaphor
for rhythms that could be joined that night:
slow, fast, faster.

I saw her an older sister, thirty-six to my twenty-one.
Chauffeured her seventeen-year-old daughter,
babysat her eight-year-old son while she dated.

On weekends, I brought rib-eye roasts from the farm.
She made Yorkshire Pudding from drippings.
We and her kids and Bob and Sharon and Big Mike reclined
stomachs full, wine bottles empty, football game droning,
eyes closed until someone woke and turned on lights.

The metaphor led to simile, even some alliteration.
Before, we plopped on the couch, leaned in without purpose.
Now a hand rested on my thigh, breath coated my neck,
a film accented by her aroma. Before I could leave,
a light bulb to change, dining room table to move,
fingernails on my back as my hands were at work.

During the graduation party, we sipped Southern Comfort.
I mulled about my future, uncertain where to go,
whether to stay. She whispered:
*You're my favorite horse, wish you'd get in the race.*
Her work-study secretary Lisa and I danced,
too drunk for steady steps, kissing in a corner:
soft, deep, deeper.

In the morning in the guest bedroom, she found Lisa and me,
clothes strewn about the floor, sheets covering our knees.
I woke for a moment, saw her smile,
a plea to be happy for us for her for the wet sheets.

I split to explore Wisconsin-Green Bay.

She did teach me this, a fragment of her New Orleans girlhood:
While chewing a divine meal, mouth dancing, declare:
*Tastes so good, you gotta cross your legs to eat it.*

## Splinter

### I

The willow house windows, one shuttered by branches
on white nights. A maul's wedge in my palm,
split oak on the sweet spot, weightless.

Stove stoked by balled want ads and tinder teepee.
We lay a quilt at the brick hearth, firebox open.
You free lacquer pins—hair tumbles down your back.

### II

Your mother escalates echoes into ear-splitting screams.
Your father and I escape to the ice field, roll stumps uphill,
nurse a six pack set in snow until we hear oaks creak.

He and I brave the door—arms filled with birch logs.
You and she glare at a shattered end table.
We build a pyre, lay the remains cross hissing limbs.

### III

A stroke breaks your mother, her words jumble like shredded bark.
She's moved to a nursing home, nests in bed,
wonders why day is dark, why trees stand bare in summer.

She wants lunch *now*, nibbles mints squirreled under her pillow.
You point—9:00 am clock—she crows *liar*.
You slam the door—panel splits clean down the center.

## At sixteen on a balmy August day,

I gallop bareback, a filly named Sally, matching her movement—
weightless, face whipped by mane, nose filling with musky sweat,
leather, manure. Sally's hooves, throbbing claps. Blinding sun—

      My shoulder bounces off rock, face splays in nettles, nose
bleeds. Still. People stand in horseshoe around me, lips moving.

                Sally saw coiled snake, bucked.

Dragged to feet, let go, caught when knees betray. Tossed on Sally's
back behind trail boss Cindy. Hug Cindy around breasts. Clip-clop
back to stable. Lean against manure heap, nap. Cindy hands me
bourbon, bug juice, 3 Musketeers. Walk arm-in-arm to supper. Table
mates complain. Fertile smell overwhelms mystery meat, grape nut
pudding.

Cindy hauls me to bunkhouse. Next morning—swollen nose, right
cheek purple, shoulder black-red-yellow. Shake my skull, hobble to
stalls, muck. Feed horses hay, oats. Dump water trough, refill with
hose.

            Mount Sally.
            Ride hillocks' haze.

## 77 Sunset Slick

14 years old, want to drive a sleek T-Bird,
be a parking lot attendant,
snap fingers at passing groovy girls.
 Comb my pompadour in a wave like Kookie.

Too young for a learners permit,
careers on hold for navigation of 8th grade,
fingers too slim to snap and turn heads.
But my hair—thick, kinky, misbehaving.

Dad sent me to a stylist,
a new breed, not to be confused with barbers.
Hair washed in a guillotine notched sink,
blades to trim locks, layering, conditioners.

Granger whistled, his fingers strutted,
blending shampoo with zig zag flair,
palpating my skull, scratching tangles
rinsing with pulses of hot water,

chatting as he edged his comb to curl.
His straight razor nipped, hair fell.
He asked if I would model for him
at Copley Place, just one Saturday,

an afternoon exhibition.
His wife and three toddlers
would stay home. Too much
commotion at a competition!

Mom nixed the adventure, sat me down,
explained that I had to be careful
around stylists and their like.
I nodded knowingly, feigned awareness.

A month later, Granger mentioned a meeting,
an opportunity to make good money
*helping people, though some may disagree.*
He wrote down the date and place.

I never showed, never returned for styling,
didn't understand Mom but an ache lingered—
I did miss his hands massaging
my shoulders, nails kneading my head

## St. Louis heat burst

At my apartment, you grab a six-pack of Busch Bavarian,
tune the TV to *Mary Hartman, Mary Hartman*.
We pile pillows against the wall
at the head of the bed.

Lounging, sipping beer, Mary Hartman
segues into a Marx Brothers movie.
You coax your head onto my shoulder.
I angle my cheek to swim in your hair.

We giggle at Harpo, agree he has the best lines.
I plant wet kisses along your neck.
Your fingernails caress my chest.
We roll across the bed until we gasp for air.

You grin, crinkle your nose.
We submerge. Hands traverse
swells and hollows, follow ridges—
collar bone crest, xylophone ribs.

Shirts, bra, fall away.
I trace your nipples with my tongue,
brush the path from heart to belly button.
Undo the top button of your jeans.

You stiffen. I look up. You smooth
my hair back, whisper *Please don't.*
I nod,
watch your teeth unclench,
rest my cheek on your tummy.

## Möbius strip

Figures the room would be on Lower Level 7.
LL1 is x-ray, MRI, imaging.
LL2 radiation oncology.
I don't care about the rest.
You told me not to think of them until I was there.
And now, I'm here. And so are you.

Figure this room for 28 degrees Fahrenheit.
Not too cold to freeze, ideal temp to preserve.
   Preserve.
Never thought a warehouse job would prepare me for this.
You never went in the freezers when you visited me at work.
   Didn't want to catch a chill.
   At least I have the proper clothing.
I brought your red roller suitcase with supplies.
Hope you approve. I'm doing this for you, not me.

Let me help you dress.
Pick up your right foot—wait you can't do that.
   A little corpse humor. Ok, I'll stop.
   You're rolling your eyes, giving me that look.
   I can never draw your humor line.
   Often you guffaw.
   Other times—well, I've learned to learn.
Up to the waist, to the scars I kiss when you feel blue—
     C-section.
     Emergency diverticulitis surgery.
     Ostomy reversal "procedure".
Like the tracks in Monet's *Field At Gennevilliers*
   I tell you they are beautiful but you don't believe me.
   They are you, our life, the hard challenges.

I brought the shell dress—ok not a formal choice,
   but neither are we. Makes me see your smile.
   You wear it loose, flowing.
You step in to don it. So, bottom up I'll go.
   Usually I just zip.

First I'll tuck the top into tight folds.
Left foot up, slide the dress, right foot, slide.
Bend my knees (only lifting with my legs, dear).

Hmm. Wish you could make a suggestion here.
Guess I will lift you up into a seating position.
Your head in my hands.         God, I love you.
       I will only be able to talk to you
          without getting a reply.

Balancing your head on my stomach, walking you up.
Cheek on my shoulder—breasts point to the door.
     Body language's different after death.
Ok. Pulling on the dress. Pick up your right arm.
     Age spots, your constellations.
     Pull the sleeve over. Now the left.
Holding you around the collarbone with my left arm.
     Reach in back for the zipper with my right hand.
     Good thing I mastered one hand zippering.
Lay you down gently. Should have brought that fox pillow.

Here are your favorite woven sandals.
Too bad they only come in Lion color.
Sole marked with the shape of your foot,
     an impression of gravity, sweat, never polish.
Toe nails cut short, rounded tops in sympathy with tips.
Flesh removed along big toes, not cosmetic,
     but to avoid ingrowth.
It's easy—won't say painless—to cup your heel,
     slip on the left, now the right.
     Don't even have to loosen the straps.

When we first met, your hair was long and silky,
     either over the shoulders or a pony tail.
Since the boys were little, it's been short.
Sometimes Talia got a little too creative with haircuts.
     You'd talk about finding someone new, but
     would have her "fix it". I was never much help.
     Your hair looks fetching to me, even when we wake.

I'll brush it out. Thought about a spray bottle and a hair dryer.
        Don't trust myself and imagine you asking *why?*
Easy to comb, straight and fine. Sometimes, you tried
        curly or a perm, but I prefer the natural look.
        Ok, I only said I liked the new styles.
Have your mascara and lipstick. Feel confident about the lips.
In what world does me applying mascara sound worthy?
We all have our talents.
        Coloring within the lines is not mine.
        We'll skip mascara. You never need it.


My feet are cold but not as cold as yours.
This dressing seemed a vast task. It's done.
Yet, I stand here waiting to put on more clothes—or—
        straighten your fingers—or—adjust your hem.
Wait. I have to check the tag in the back of the dress.
That is my grave responsibility. Make certain it's tucked in.
            I will miss that.


I'm a lingerer. Last to leave a party or meeting.
        You like heading home while the room's still full.
        Don't have you to keep me from milling in place.


We used to joke about who would be the dresser
        and who the dressee,
        who the mourner, who sleeping.
Guess we won't be able to debate which is the harsher task.
        I mean, I'll talk to you all day about this,
        especially when I'm in the kitchen with a sponge,
        looking out the window at the crab apple tree,
        feeling water drip down my arm soaking my shirt.
There must be something more.

## An Assignation with Death
~ after "How to Stay Warm in Heaven" by Sara Nicholson

your fingers, no more bones than my bones onions
in the pale of orgasm, I seek to hide from you

imagine my skin dried, face a skull, back nailed to bed
you ride a black stallion, snaked around the saddle horn

painless to leave the earth when living equals pain
terror to exit the garden running a personal best

breath starts bartering for days, an illusion of air
destined for the grave, knuckles tapping waltzes on pine

## Memorial Day

"He doesn't have seasons enough to have
a season for every purpose. Ecclesiastes
Was wrong about that."
~ "A Man Doesn't Have Time In His Life" by Yehudi Amichai

In cemeteries, we kick dirt, strain grass, dig mud,
search for pebbles to adorn headstones.

Hallowed ground—pocked, fallow, picked.
Stones left by flag planters, grave sweepers—

open season for grifters too lazy to forage.
From gated homes, they laud today's warriors—

strangers' kids deployed to gravel kill zones.
They steal stones to offer as their own.

# Uncle Louie
## wonders if the North Star
## is leading him astray

"Your old men shall dream dreams,
your young men shall see visions."
~ Joel 2:28


"You're the smart one. Why didn't you tell me life was a dream?"
~ Allen Ginsberg, in a letter to Jack Kerouac

## Preamble

These poems are a work of fiction. Any misconceptions, irregularities, or non-abiding witticisms are wholly the author's fault. What truth inhabits these tales springs from the author's memory. However, the author's memory is quite faulty, prone to exaggeration, and more than a bit disingenuous.

These poems concern my Great-Uncle Louie, henceforth referred to as Uncle Louie as is the habit of all generations of our family. He was ageless but always old to me. Uncle Louie was the guy you wanted to go out on the town with whether you were five, fifteen, or fifty-five years old. An adventure was brewing. Laughter would follow. Rules were suspended. You were strutting the Boardwalk with Uncle Louie. Believe it!

The basis of the later poems in this series come from experiences I shared with Uncle Louie and from family legends. There were often sundry details that needed filling in and the author let his imagination run as wild as Uncle Louie lived. I wrote these later poems first but began wondering who Uncle Louie was as a child immigrating from White Russia, as a boy in the schoolyard. What did Uncle Louie do before joining the Navy? How was he disabled? I began reverse-engineering Uncle Louie's life, taking defining characteristics and imagining what experiences shaped them.

There is no family history about Uncle Louie's years in the Navy. He never spoke of World War I. Some describe him as a simple man yet I watched him perform arithmetic feats in seconds (most of these feats had to do with trifectas, odds, and payouts from Racing Forms but they were magnificent.)

I wonder if Uncle Louie would enjoy these poems. I think so. I hope so. He was beloved while being the joker at any event. What would happen? He wouldn't...well, I guess he did.

Uncle Louie, grab a 'Gansett, a shot of Crown Royal, a Dutch Masters Corona Deluxe Natural, and read these poems. I await your response.

## 1. Uncle Louie learns a shipmate's ropes on the voyage from White Russia to the land where streets are paved with gold

Uncle Louie, eight years old,
>slips away from Aunt Yitta in steerage,
>wanders passageways, ladders, decks
>peers into the engine room,
Simon the sailor grabs his collar, drags him to the poop deck.
>*Stay out of there, runt. Ya ain't got sea legs, might*
>*bump into a boiler. Burn ya skin like bacon on a grille.*

Uncle Louie shadows Simon, carries tubs of wash,
>hangs laundry on lines, learns to spit high over rails.
Crew laugh at his accent but feed him words,
>teach him how to tie knots, roll cigarettes,
>hide from officers, throw dice, beat a cut deck.

Tossed by typhoon's waves, Simon feeds him white bread.

Uncle Louie coughs, burns with croup.
>Simon pulls whiskey from a hidden panel,
>steals aspirin from the dispensary.
>Uncle Louie gargles, swallows, sleeps.
>His fever breaks.

Above the bridge on a wide beam,
>Uncle Louie tracks constellations, listens.
>Captain and First Mate smoke cigars, talk their talk.
>*We'll raid Simon's whiskey stash tomorrow.*
>*Toss the braggart in the brig, bread and water.*

Uncle Louie waits for officer's morning mess,
>sneaks through shadows, pulls bottles
>from the panel into a potato sack.
Uncle Louie takes the back ladder to steerage,
>slides the sack into Yitta's trunk,
>covers it with delicates.
The officers march Simon to the panel—
>open it—find dead air.

Uncle Louie catches Simon's eye, winks.

Last day of the voyage, Simon glides his pinky ring—gold,
       blue garnet—onto Uncle Louie's middle finger.
       They share a cigarette at the bow rail.
       Rainbows glint off white caps.

Uncle Louie disembarks beneath the Statue's gaze.
       Under his choppy steps, Ellis Island sways.

### 3. Uncle Louie feels his sea legs ripple

Uncle Louie slashes a carcass, loses his job at Minkins Meats.
Finds day work loading crates of fish into sea containers.
Too many newspaper columns, even Yiddish, urge for Prohibition.
Maybe if he didn't gulp nips, he wouldn't be fired so frequently.

A horn pulls every eye to the ship entering the harbor:
The USS Michigan, one of the new dreadnought battleships.
Uncle Louie watches the crew ballet from station-to-station.
Old Glory snaps in the wind. White uniforms glow in morning light.

Uncle Louie leaves the pier for lunch break, trails sailors,
young men, crisp blouses, laughing, walking with legs bowed.
He looks down at his coveralls stained with fish guts.
Simon's garnet ring on his right pinky glares.

The seamen jut their jaws into each other's faces when joking.
They salute, then mutter at an officer crossing their path.
Uncle Louie thinks of Simon running the rigging,
teaching him how to carve canes, lures, goblins.

Uncle Louie strides the length of the Michigan, reads her flags,
admires her lattice mast, super firing twin gun turrets.
A Petty Officer, creased garrison cap, marches by, nods.
Uncle Louie sets his legs, feels the deck glide under his feet.

## 4. Uncle Louie sees the tide turn but gets caught in the rip current

Uncle Louie, home on leave, first port: Schwartz's Delicatessen.
Mendel greets him at the door. They pound shoulders, pull noses.
*Mendela, you look well. Married life agrees with you, no?*

"Leybish, you're a rock. Look at that muscle! No tummy.
You need some fatty corned beef, latkes, rugelach."
Uncle Louie pulls up a sleeve, flashes a tight bicep.
Mendel slides the sleeve higher, a Navy insignia tattoo.

*Shhhh. Don't tell. Mamé will find out when I'm dead. Maybe.*
*Listen, I smuggled in single-malt. Let's fill four coke bottles,*
*strut the Boardwalk. Ride the rides blotto.*

Mendel shakes his head. "Leybish, Perle and Herman
will be expecting us for dinner. Perle's making a brisket,
honey cake. And that's not all she has in the oven!
Herman will be a big brother soon."

Uncle Louie sighs. *Guess I best not bring the hootch.*
*How you doing? Your father still have you cleaning toilets?*

"I've moved up in the world. I roast all the meats now.
Put together catering orders. Make sandwiches sometimes.
Tâte says one day the deli will be mine. He's a happy Zady.
What about you, Leybish? Are you staying in the Navy?"

Uncle Louie rubs the three stripes and crow on his blouse.
*Mendela, I wake up every morning to crashing waves.*
*And—there's a war brewing. My men need me.*

*In White Russia, I was fodder. Look at me.*
*A Chief. A gentleman. I'm rarin' to fight the Krauts.*
*If I die, don't be sad. I won't be. Just bury me at sea.*
*Mamé won't be happy—but the tattoo is a shande far di kinder.*

## 5. Uncle Louie tracks his mentor to a sick bay

Uncle Louie's ship anchors—His Majesty's Naval Base, Portsmouth.
For Shore Leave, he journeys north to Widley, Simon's hometown,
finds The George Inn, the pub featured in late night tales.

Uncle Louie pulls up a stool, slides his hand on the oak top,
admires the wide grain, sees the reflection of his garrison cap.
The landlord eyes his stripes, nods, *What will it be, Chief?*

Uncle Louie removes his cap, spots the rows of taps, bottles.
*A pint of your best local ale, a dram of your favorite whiskey.*
*If you'd like to join me, pour a round for yourself, my treat.*

They toast the King, the President, The Royal Navy, The US Navy.
Uncle Louie asks *I have an old friend from Widley, Simon Bell.*
*You know his family?* The landlord refills the whiskey glasses.

*Yeah, I know the family. Know Simon. We were school mates.*
*He liked to mix it up, always in trouble. Made me laugh.*
*He's in a bad way now. Cancer. Royal Portsmouth Hospital.*

Uncle Louie pays his tab, adds five pence, thanks the landlord.
Takes a cab to the hospital, stops to buy a pint of rum.
A nurse leads him across a ward larger than a barracks to a bed.

Uncle Louie looks down at a shriveled body, face all bone.
Simon's green eyes sparkle. *Little Louis. Am I dreaming?*
*Have I died? You're the big one now. A Petty Officer!*

Simon bites his lip, holds his stomach, stifles a feral wail.
*You always pop up. Where I'm not expecting you.*
*What has it been. Fifteen years, twenty? Still wear my ring?*

Uncle Louie holds up his right hand, bounces light off garnet.
*Middle to pointer to ring to pinkie. I've carried you with me.*
*Was hoping we'd tip a few at The George Inn. Guess that's out.*
*Brought a pint of Pusser's Rum. We can toast the old days.*

Simon coughs. *Sorry, shipmate…I'm a bloody sack of bones.*
*Can't sit up. Even with laudanum. Tell you what.*
*Wet my lips. Take a slug for you. A slug for me.*
*I get a taste. You get a double. I watch.*

Uncle Louie wets the ring pinky with rum, leans over Simon,
tenderly coats his lips, twice. Takes two healthy swigs himself.
He holds Simon's hand in his. They sit in silence.
Simon closes his eyes. Uncle Louie waits.

## 6. Uncle Louie watches one get away

Navy trousers, two months after disability discharge—
they don't plunge in the wind, pinch the crotch.
Civie white shirt does have more pockets.

Uncle Louie limps post to post along the boardwalk,
stops to rub his knee, pull his calf straight—
a grimace, a slug of rye whiskey.
He flips the flask to read the front
      "Bottoms up shipmate!
      Don't take no
      wooden nickels."

He lights a Dutch Masters,
leans on the rail, dreams into whitecaps.
Clouds roil by at a good clip.
Beach fades, ocean crashes—
slate sky to the northeast.
High seas splatter gun mounts

on the horizon, a destroyer under full steam.
*Ahoy! Fair winds and following seas.*
Uncle Louie empties his flask,
sits on the edge of planks,
feet rock in time with the dip of the mast.
He spits into the wind,
saliva whips back onto his cheek

No sea legs, just a bum shank.
The deck doesn't move with the sea

# 7. Uncle Louie, late for battle, stomps the decks

Uncle Louie chugs beer with Mendel after the day shift.
Home, he climbs the first flight of stairs, steps on a broken
dairy bottle, double-times the next two flights towing his leg,

arrives at the open apartment door, eggs strewn about foyer.
Ida sweeps up a china platter. *We were robbed. But I caught him.*
Uncle Louie, hands in fists, storms through the apartment,

reaches under his headboard, slips out a nightstick.
*Shvester, are you hurt? What did the ganef steal?*
Ida pats him on the cheek. *I came home from marketing. He was here.*

*In my pillowcase, MY pillowcase, our money and silver.*
*I swung my pocketbook. Smashed his nose.*
*Kicked him in the beytsim. He dropped the pillowcase,*

*started to run out the door. I threw eggs. Then a milk bottle.*
*Knocked him down the stairs. From the porch, I saw Mendel's sons.*
*Yelled to them. They tackled, dragged him to the corner.*

*Waved to a policeman. A paddy wagon came.*
*A detective came. Asked me lots of questions. Laughed.*
*I just wanted to clean.*

Uncle Louie paces the length of the apartment three times.
Sits on the couch, rolls the nightstick in his hands, growls.
*Nu, erst vos tut mir, Shvester? Should I go to the station?*

*Bruder, he got nothing. We lost groceries. The platter broke.*
*Mr. Detective told me he's Jewish. I dropped charges.*
*Leave him alone. I don't want any more trouble in my home.*

Uncle Louie hugs Ida, slides the nightstick under his left arm.
Smokes four cigarettes outside the police station.
The ganef hobbles out, hand on groin, nose caked with blood.

Uncle Louie follows him two blocks, slaps nightstick to palm,
recalls as a child, how his ears rung when Ida boxed them,
how he sprinted to hide in answer to her bellowing.

Uncle Louie turns right, meanders past the VFW bar,
climbs the Boardwalk's observation tower, closes his eyes,
heeds the waves crashing into the breakwater.

## 8. Uncle Louie schools his nephews in proper nighttime deportment

Uncle Louie, 2 am, staggers home from pinochle,
pisses a three minute waterfall,
tosses his "west" on the bed in his chamber.

Limping into his nephews' room,
he bugles his nose into a silk handkerchief.
Three boys in one bed pop up, rub their eyes.

*What, you had a farting contest? Oy veyzmir!*
*Go to my "west", take all the quarters you want.*
Uncle Louie holds no stead for pennies, nickels, dimes.

But four bits buys Schwartz's blue plate special:
brisket, latkes with apple sauce, cole slaw,
pickles and green tomatoes, cream soda.

Uncle Louie pours a nightcap,
swaggers onto the porch, collapses
into a lounger, feet on the railing.

## 16. Uncle Louie stands watch over his great-nephews

Nathan and I grab our guitars, car keys.
Uncle Louie sits in the foyer, reads *The Jewish Advocate*.
I ask *do you want anything from the store? cigars?*
He looks at torn jeans, Beatle and Stones t-shirts,
my drivers license a week old.
Uncle Louie spouts *what are you two up to?*

*We're going to Preston Beach, play music, meet girls.*
Uncle Louie folds the newspaper, shuffles it under his arm,
limps to the front door, stares. *Why the store?*

*We're going to get a six-pack of soda,*
*pretzels, jumbo sack of popcorn.*
He shakes his head, expels a whistling breath.

*Argh. You two are gonna try to get some beer,*
*head over to Harold King Forest, hide.*
*I better buy it for you so you don't get in trouble.*

## 11. Uncle Louie sets a course but loses his compass

Uncle Louie meets The Gal at Schwartz's Delicatessen.
From his back corner booth, he can watch the door, signal a waiter.
Tables and counter full, she asks to join him.
Eating fatty pastrami on rye, twin to his sandwich,
she talks about her job, an unwed sister in the family way.
They mimic Lester Allen & Nellie Breen's Burlesque routine.
Uncle Louie picks up her check—invites her to the pictures.

The Gal, on his arm, ringside at the fights,
straightens his tie, holds his derby in her lap.
At the horse track, Uncle Louie interprets the racing form.
She bets Grace O' Malley across the board, filly places.
The Gal coaxes him to see Tommy Dorsey at the Beachview.
They dance in a dark corner, his leg drags, she twirls—smiles.
In the opera house, her eyes fill with tears, she mouths an aria.
Uncle Louie's years on dog watches keep him awake.

The Gal bakes marble cake, sour cream frosting for his birthday.
Gives him a blue cardigan, a dozen pairs of white postal socks.
They sip a fifth of rye until it's dry at midnight.
Uncle Louie tells her the stories he's told no one.
The years in the Navy, losing men to the sea, to fire.
The night his leg shattered—ink darkness, torrid flashes.
They fall asleep in each other's arms under the duvet.

Uncle Louie's mother picks his underwear off the floor daily.
His paycheck disappears at the track, in poker games.
More than once, a week goes by without calling on The Gal.
Valentines Day, he watches a new man hand her a bouquet.
Uncle Louie gulps bourbon, passes out on the beach.
He wears the postal socks after they no longer hold his ankles.
The cardigan, layered with stains, frayed at the elbows,
covers his pajama top on his last night, to his last breath.

## 12. Uncle Louie visits his niece after her surgery for women's problems

Why did she go all the way to Newton-Wellesley?
Might as well be New York City. Or Miami Beach.
Had to call Herman for a ride.
Little pisher's home on leave. A Lieutenant Commander.
Squared away. I'd be taking orders from him. Saluting.
Got a dozen pink roses. Forty ounce Whitman's Sampler.
Ha! Herman and his dress whites are dropping back.
Face red. He's hunting a hideaway.
Time to croon to all the pretty nurses, make 'em smile.
*Stand Navy down the field, sails set to the sky...*

What's that racket? Sounds like a marching band. Oy vey—
Uncle Louie is here. Only one man can make that much noise.
He can't drive. Won't take buses. Wonder how he got here.
No one on this corridor will sleep. He's howling shanties.
There he is, grinning in the doorway. Flowers, bonbons—
always candy for kinder by the pound. Five limps to the bed.
He nudges a chair near, gentle kiss on my forehead,
bouquet softly laid on my right, chocolates on my left.
Uncle Louie holds my hand, jokes. Poor Herman blushes.
Kisses my cheek. Shoulder squeeze. Herm does love Louie.

### 13. Uncle Louie ushers me through The Revere Beach Boardwalk rides

Uncle Louie clasps my hand in his left,
       draws my shoulder to his waist,
his right holds a smoldering Dutch Masters,

racing form under the arm.
       He buys me a double chocolate cone.
I eat and walk, catch drips with my shirt.

Uncle Louie sips a 'Gansett from a Red Sox cup,
       dribbles beer onto his navy sweater.
I spin toward The Whip, frown at the height sign—

Uncle Louie pats the carny on the back.
       The carny laughs, pockets a palmed bill
waves me on with a family of four.

I mount an Arabian stallion on the Merry-Go-Round,
       Uncle Louie looks up from his racing form,
shakes his cigar at me, circles a pony's name.

I dismount to a box of popcorn, a milkshake.
       We pause at the hundred foot tall Cyclone Coaster:
MINORS MUST BE ACCOMPANIED BY AN ADULT!

Its operator doesn't laugh, pushes money away.
       Uncle Louie surveys the crowd, grabs my arm,
he whistles at four Seamen, yells *Attention on deck!*

Uncle Louie wades into the middle of them,
       talks the talk, straightens garrison caps.
One of the Seamen nods *I'll take him, Chief.*

The Cyclone climbs, rocks at the top, plunges.
       Four-leaf-clover green streams from my mouth.
The Seaman holds my head over the rail.

*It's ok, Chief. Rates high on the Clinometer.*
   Uncle Louie passes me a caramel apple, a root beer,
sips a sweating bottle of Schaefer.

*Uncle Louie, Nana's making supper.*
    *Maybe I should wait. Save this for dessert.*

*Nah kid. You can eat pot roast and potatoes anytime.*
    *Today you're struttin' The Boardwalk with me.*

### 15. Uncle Louie transforms boychikels into shtarkers

I.
Mendel of Schwartz's Deli pumps Uncle Louie's hand,
seats him, us five lambs in the corner booth.

*Leybish, want the usual?* Uncle Louie belches.
*Yep. Pastrami—fatty—on rye with brown mustard.*

*Give the boys cream sodas, me a bottle of Schlitz.*
*Don't forget extra half sours and green tomatoes.*

I whisper *Uncle Louie, Tommy doesn't eat meat.*
*What? Is his zipper on the side of his pants, too?*

II.
Ringside seats at the fights. Uncle Louie slips a fin
to a stogie smoker who scribbles in a notebook.

Black man in red trunks crushes Kraut boxer's nose,
crude crack, blood sprays on the canvas—on us.

Uncle Louie confides *schwartze, strong as bear!*
After the round, the spit bucket spills on our Keds.

Tommy keels over, retches relish onto concrete.
*Shmendrik! Lucky he didn't eat the pastrami.*

## 17. Uncle Louie asks me for a lift home but first braces himself for the voyage

Uncle Louie nudges my shoulder
*I'm almost done, kid. Wait here.*

He starts from the port side
of the Bar Mitzvah parents' table

chugs the balance of each libation
careful not to swallow cigarette butts—

he grimaces when a Whiskey Sour
follows a White Russian.

The starboard end: scotch neat with date pits
sipped through a frosted dessert fork.

Uncle Louie wipes his mouth on the tablecloth
burps, kisses his sister and nieces good night.

*C'mon kid. Time to weigh anchor.*
He's snoring before we clear the harbor.

## 19. Uncle Louie follows a hunch at Suffolk Downs and screws the pooch

Uncle Louie spies Splendid Splinter hoofing hay.
This quarter horse's hind limb muscles ripple.

He peers in the paddock, an eye stares back unblinking,
dun mask, black stripe cross the withers, zebra legs.

Racing form warns DQs, false favorites, lunges.
Uncle Louie, in love, puts his last yard on the nose.

Splendid Splinter, front runner at the first turn.
Head of the stretch, head hung, he starts climbing.

At the last pole, he flattens out, falls to the rear.
Uncle Louie snaps his stub, tears it into fours.

Back at the apartment, packets of saltines, mustard.
Dregs of flat beer wash it down.

## 21. Uncle Louie hits the rack

Uncle Louie hobbles onto his balcony,
plops on the end of a casting couch,
turns gingerly, leans back on an attached pillow.

The plastic fabric, sour—cracked—spitting water.
His body, weeks removed from a shower—
skin peeling—skivvies stained yellow.

Uncle Louie pulls a cigar from his shirt pocket.
Slices the tip, tosses it over the rail at a seagull.
A lighter slides out his shorts. He flicks the wheel,

fires up a Dutch Master, inhales, coughs.
Inhales again, hacks phlegm, fills a handkerchief.
The cigar dies, needs breaths. He flips it in a can.

Uncle Louie closes his eyes. On a destroyer—
rotgut, hand-rolled butts, six racks per berth.
His veteran digs—roomier than captains quarters.

Rye scorches the stomach. He abandons his flask.
Waves crash into rocks below, deck steady until
he rises, dizzy—hands paw walls—legs shake.

## 22. Uncle Louie makes friends at the West Roxbury VA Hospital

The doctor recommends removal of a testicle—
         no misunderstanding.
         I enfold Uncle Louie as he leaps, bellows
         60 years younger, my shoes hold the deck.

Around the day room's linoleum table, six play pinochle—
         toothpicks in the pot
         no ashtrays
         no hidden flasks.

I notice Uncle Louie's tokus peek out his johnnie,
         ask how he's doing.

*I'm sitting with a bunch of cripples playing cards for sticks.*
*How d'ya think I'm doing?*

The other players fold

## 23. Uncle Louie directs us what to salvage from his quarters now that he berths at the VA hospital

Uncle Louie spurns the VA wheelchair,
lays in bed, beads of sweat fleck his forehead.

He reveals which magazine hides the winning stubs.
We are charged with collecting his proceeds from the track.
—bring him six sets skivvies, three button down shirts, two trousers
—trash the rest but don't let the janitor pinch the TV.

Dad & I ride an elevator built for two.
Uncle Louie's digs—apartment 711—his home
for decades, family never encroached its threshold.
Invitations, cards, gifts mailed to an anonymous address.

Under the table—undatable palette of crumbs.
Over couch cushions—shirts, pants, trash bags.
Coffee table layered—Peacoat, derby hat, gloves.
Strewn about floor—socks, underpants, sleeveless tees.

We pack the clothes in a carpet bag.
Unveiled in a drawer—a dozen brand new dress shirts—
in plastic, pinned, collars' integrity warranted by cardboard.
The labels read 'Gift from Shack's', our hometown store.

Before the track, we pause for a glance from the porch.
Below: waves batter barnacle freckled rocks,
southward: Boston Harbor's bulge, whitecaps,
northward: Revere Beach's four-mile silver crescent.

Dad would say *Poor man, stuck in that dark hole.*
Uncle Louie spun, scored three Liberty Bells—
a view never flaunted.

## 24. Uncle Louie maneuvers The Seven Seas, The US Navy, The Great War

circumnavigating his deathbed, we wonder—

      was his ship struck by a Kraut torpedo?
          did he drag a leg riddled with shrapnel
          to man a firehose? trigger depth charges?
      aim a Springfield at the surrendering sub crew?
      or
      after poker & grog, did he topple off a teetered ladder?
          have shipmates hoist him to his rack?
          later to a duty station for morning watch
      where he lurched on a recoiling deck, ripped up a knee?

did Uncle Louie man the rails out of Pearl
      a full war before The Day of Infamy?

counsel a green swabbie during a typhoon,
      *eat white bread, fill your stomach*?

      At the graveside service, a Chief plays taps
          on a boombox, intones
          *this flag...symbol... appreciation...your*
      *loved one...service...Country...grateful Navy.*

      Uncle Louie's great-great-nephew accepts the flag,
          slips it into a triangle case, returns a salute,
          calls out *Splice the Main Brace*. We toast rye,
      smash anchor-etched glasses against granite.

# Divrei Torah

"I would like…to see us take hold of ourselves,
look at ourselves, and cease being afraid."
~ Eleanor Roosevelt


"Be still when you have nothing to say;
when genuine passion moves you,
say what you've got to say, and say it hot."
~ D.H. Lawrence

# On the nature of knuckles and knives

*The first thing is to clean the knife.*
*Always the first thing.*
Wimpy hands me a white rag.
I polish the 8-inch cleaver. Fine German steel.

*Güt. Now use the stone to test the edge.*
*Shimmy both sides.*
I slide the edge carefully down the stone.
Twice for each side, careful to avoid pitting.
I could shave with this—if I had a beard.

*Pick a cold cooked lobster off the cart.*
*If the body is warm, dunk it in ice.*
The one chosen, about a pound and a
quarter, chills my hand.

*Gloves—without them, you shred your hands.*
I jam my fingers deep into heavy rubber.

*Grab your lobster.*
*Put your right hand around the tail.*
*Pull up until you hear it break and separate.*
Through the glove, I feel the shell's grooves.
I grip, pull up, the tail loosens with a crack.
It falls free.

*Turn the tail over.*
*Push the fins down hard.*
*When they snap, pull 'em away.*
The fins fall apart more easily than I expect.

*Güt. Now turn the tail back up,*
*clasp and squeeze until the ribs break.*
My palms surround the tail.
I press hard, thinking my hands nutcrackers.
A smooth series of pops. The carapace shatters.

*Flip the tail down.*
*Strip the shell from the pods.*
The exoskeleton opens like a pencil box.

*Shake the tail meat out—careful, one clean piece.*
*Don't nick it or we can only sell it in salad.*
I gently goad the shell side-to-side.
The tail drops into my hand like an orphan.
I place it in the tail tin.

*Hold a claw in your fist, rip up and back.*
*It will pull away from the body.*
A sound like splitting wood
announces the severed claw.
Vibrations tingle my forearm.

*Güt. Now be careful. I want you to take the cleaver,*
*make diagonal slits here, here, here, and here.*
*But you mustn't cut past the shell. All shell, no meat.*
*Or we use it for salad and lose money.*
Am I being careful not to damage the flesh
  or not to remove one of my fingers?
   Guess either could make salad.
I keep my wrist loose and grip firm.
My left hand aligns the target.
A quick flip, like hitting a stapler, firm but gentle.
The shell cracks.
There is empty space between my cut and the meat.
I cleave the claw again, the knuckle twice.

*Very Güt! Now wipe your knife,*
*always wipe your knife before the next thing.*
I run a rag over the edge, spray a little water
to remove cartilage, wipe the blade clean.
The cloth shreds.

*Now this is the slippery part.*
*Peel the shell off the claws and knuckles.*
*Watch yourself.*
*We want the meat in one piece.*
*Oh, and the shell is sharp.*
*Can cut you through the gloves.*
The shell edge pinches the heavy rubber.
I tear the slits to the shell's sides, expose the claw.
      Carefully slice it away from the knuckles
      with a fillet knife tucked in my apron sleeve.
I flip the claw into the claw tin then wipe the knife.

*Güt! The knuckles are the best meat.*
*Toss the bodies into a crate—we sell them too.*
*Hector is bringing out a cart with 100 lobsters.*
*Clean those. Then you go for lunch.*
*After you wipe and oil your knives.*

As carefully as I peel the knuckle, I feel my skin gouge.
I shake the knuckles out and place them in the knuckle tin.

## Old Country remedies

I.
croupy child cries from crib
mix    one shot boiling water
       one shot Schnapps
       tablespoon of honey
stir    child gargles, swallows
       sleeps

II.
for a thick mane
to arrest balding
       shave the skull to a shine
       rub urine into the roots
turn girls' heads

## Wallpaper peeling above the headboard

Granny dying
sent me away
*don't want him seeing me like this*
I'll never forget
the bedspread's silver threads

## December 7 on the Cusp of The Millennium
~ Random lives share day of birth

Host and Guests:
Ida Cohen Fox—my paternal grandmother, three sons served in
        WWII, beloved of Meyer
Solomon Schechter—Talmudic scholar, founder of American
        Conservative Jewry
Akiko Yosano—Poet, Peace & Women's Rights Activist,
        founder of Women's College
Akiko's grandson—Imperial Japanese Navy pilot
Sailor—turned 20 on the USS Arizona

"Awake ye dreamers…" Knuckles knock wood. Rubber heals rap
kitchen floor, pad carpet. A glance to the table—teapot, soup kettle,
Shirley Avenue bakery boxes on linen cloth. Nana Ida straightens her
black gown, slides the deadbolt, turns the brass knob.

Solomon Schechter touches fingertips to the Mezuzah, to his lips,
strokes a salt and pepper beard.  His palms trace a black coat, follow
tallis to severed fringes. He cups Ida's hands. "In Job it is written
*Where is the way where light dwelleth? and as for darkness, where is the place
thereof?* So we five gather on our day of birth." Solomon sits in Zady
Meyer's chair, head of the table.

Akiko Yosano bows, her white gown a pool bathing Ida's feet. She
massages Ida's shoulders. *"To punish men for their endless sins, god gave me
this fair skin, this long black hair."* Akiko eases into the chair to
Schechter's left.

Ida pulls a young Japanese man through the doorway. He removes a
fur lined pilot's helmet, bows, searches the room for Akiko. She taps
the chair next to her. "When a grandchild was born on my birthday, I
thought it was a blessing. He bombed Pearl Harbor. During the Battle
of Midway, he died in his Zero on the Akagi's deck." Akiko stokes his
cheek. *"Tears in your eyes. You ask for sympathy. I look at the waning moon
reflected on the lonely lake."*

The door is closed by the final guest, a United States sailor in blues, blouse embroidered ARIZONA. He surveys the table, glares at Akiko and the pilot. Ida rubs his back, moves him to the chair opposite the pilot. The sailor clutches a silver spoon, drums Morse Code on the table.

Nana lifts the china teapot, wide spout inlayed with mother of pearl, pours five cups. "Last year's group, Mary Queen of Scots, Giovanni Bernini, Madame Marie Tussaud, Willa Cather—were they guests or was I their cook?"

Akiko wraps her hands around the hot porcelain. "I was with Tussaud one year. She related that Cicero's head and right hand were chopped off by Mark Antony's soldiers this day."

Solomon breaths the steam. "Certainly not poetic justice though The Roman Empire may have called it poetic license. Bernini recited Cicero to me. But I prefer his vision *An architect proves his skill by turning the defects of a site into advantages.*"

Ida ladles soup into Solomon's bowl. "My great-grandsons went to one of your schools. My machatunim qvells, the kinder daven better than in the old country." She drops a second knaidlach and carrot into the broth.

"Boys, there are boxes, open them." Pilot and sailor lock eyes across the table, yank red and white string. Knots unravel in a single tug. The pilot's brown box holds marble bread, the sailor's cookies—each half chocolate, half vanilla. "Nu, pass them around."

"Arnold went to Europe, Danny was kept in California. Melvin, our youngest, was sent to Guam. But you boys wouldn't have met him. Akiko, where were your children stationed?" Ida serves each bowl without spilling a drop.

85

"My son and grandsons went to China, Russia, all over The Pacific. I spoke against war, thought I may go to prison. Ida, did you try?"

The ladle rattles. "My people were herded into camps, turned to ash. That was the silence of those years."

Nana sets the cover on the soup kettle. "Solomon, lead us."

The sailor shifts in his chair, strikes knife on napkin like a drunken drummer, waves at the pilot.

Solomon slaps the table. "Young man. *The Bible hardly contains a command bidding us to believe...nor is any punishment assigned as awaiting him who denies it.*" The sage clears his throat. "*Barukh atah Adonai, Elohaynu, melekh ha-olam ha-motzi lechem min ha-aretz. Blessed is the Lord Our G-d, King of the Universe, who makes bread from the earth.*" He reaches for a sugar cube to hold between teeth while drinking tea.

Ida chimes "Wait—the other *Berakhah!*"

Solomon is silent.

Ida chants "*Barukh atah Adonai, Elohaynu, melekh ha-olam she-hecheeyanu v'keey'manu v'heegeeyanu la-z'man ha-zeh. Blessed is the Lord Our G-d, King of the Universe, who has sustained us, and enabled us to reach this great day.*"

## Yom Kippur D'Var Torah

*Father forgive me—war limits leave.*

        *Why aren't you here in Birkenau?*
        *How does the Führer allow Juden officers?*

Son removes hat, wooden rack creaks as he sits.
Leather boots reflect skulled faces.

*Göring decides who is a Jew in the Wehrmacht,*
*but—in the heat of battle—the Shema is on my lips.*

        *A Captain now, an Iron Cross.*
        *I should be proud of my boy.*

They stare through a pine framed window, through
barbed wire, to train tracks carved into the forest.

*My Panzers lead the Blitzkrieg. Soldiers follow me through artillery,*
*machine guns. Our casualties are low. When one of my men dies,*
*I hold him in my arms, write his family, tell of the glory their son*
*bought The Fatherland. You raised me well.*

        *Your cousins Saul, Shoshana, Shira are dust.*
        *What the SS did—six year old Shira hostage*
        *to make Shoshana a whore...I wrote you—*

He coughs as the breeze turns, funnels smoke into
the barrack. From a ragged blanket, he pulls a Siddur.

*I am a Hauptmann, my influence reaches only so far.*
*You breathe, receive extra rations.*

        *Today, we read* The Binding of Isaac. *I*
        *wondered which of us is Abraham,*
        *which is Isaac.*
        *Whose voice cries out in the wilderness?*
        *Should that knife have taken the ram?*

He stands for Kedushah.
Davens, eyes on The Word.

*It is nearly dusk, I must leave.*

*My division goes to Russia tomorrow.*

## Tiananmen Tank Tamer

No one knows my name. Everyone knows my gait,
a pigeon-toed shuffle, head tilted, shoulders low.
My eyes shift in the shadow of a cannon barrel.

A plastic bag hung over my wrist shakes my hand—
plums, apples, pad with crisp white pages,
purple pen—my knees frozen pipes.

A plan—write sweet Lijuan love jueju—foiled.
Dinner—now pulp in puddles—trips me.
I roll from kicks, footprints stamped by soles.

A path, civil engineer—bridges, tunnels—failed.
This Yunnan village where Grandfather was born:
I wear a bamboo hat, grey trousers, work shirt.

In paddies, slogans pull shoots faster than fingers.
Under stars: eat, write, sleep. Conceal leaflets,
a red striped bag. Smuggle revolution with rice.

## Quảng Ngãi Café

sugared coffee
tables rattle, walking bombs

each ordnance, unique cameo in foam
rpg          poppies dance in breeze
mortar       sea fig tree shadow drifts
rocket        silhouette of mama, smiling

watch mama shudder

cousin shrieks, blood stream from temple
       sister wraps her khăn ran

wall leaks brick

every eye counts clan
       thunderclap shakes the deck
       that one, further away

baby girl, mute in bassinet
       pull back cover—sticky
       raw flesh, butchered rabbit
       nose, mouth—fountains—
       dye the white comforter

## The difference between
## life and death, 1/2 of 1%

Jason Dog scampers trails,
keeps tabs on novice hikers' lament.

Climbing mountains we haul
canvas halves of a Half-Shelter tent.

Shoulder-to-shoulder march.
*Peace Now* chant wrapped in crimson portent.

Snug steamroller flying
Stratosphere supplies the sad event.

We celebrated hard
won odds ninety-nine point five percent,

till bloody coughs declared
willful mets achieved point five's intent.

## Committing Bill's ashes to The Gulf of Mexico at 26° 28' 623" N x 82° 14' 14.402" W
~ for William Gordon Merritt, December 30, 1926—December 30, 2013

Captain Rob's Vee-Bottom boat bounces off pilings.
He winches our arms, swings us onto helm chairs,
hands the dogs, tails fluttering, down to us.
We secure gear, stow the container in watertight locker.
Cruising the NO WAKE zone, we tie hoods tight,
insulate our hands with dog fur.
Captain Rob opens the throttles,
sea spray coats our faces, wind steals beneath layers,
sweatshirts flap, balloon with salty gusts.
We wrap towels around the dogs cradled in our laps.

Three dolphins emerge from the wake,
leap, half-roll, fall back the sea,
jockey for the spot closest to the propeller.
Dog noses flex toward the revelers.
No barks, no paws urge to join the game.
We slow to navigate Redfish Pass.
Dolphins turn as one, seek deeper water.

Captain Rob drifts the roundabout to a stop,
just east of Blind Pass off Sanibel's western shore.
A funnel of sunshine peels through roiling clouds.
We open the locker, hold the container to the light.
Embossed pearl biodegradable rag, no image,
no name for sea creatures to read.
Bill's daughter slips it off port side. It follows
currents under the boat, emerges at the bow,
dances amid whitecaps, reflects rays to the heavens.

We chant the Mourners Kaddish,
beat of trope matches slapping of waves.
*Oseh shalom bimrompav, hu ya'aseh shalom*
*aleinu v'al kol-yisrael, v'imru amen.*


                        As we utter the last notes,
the container lists left, points one corner to the sky,
        pauses.
                Bill disappears in the Gulf.

## Retrieval

Oxfords   spackled with dirt
dirt   from Dad's grave
should polish   snap a rag
until I reflect off leather

wool pants   unpacked from Paris
Paris   last heard   his voice
on the phone   told him *home Tuesday*
he replied *can't wait to see you*

Tuesday   eight hour flight
two hour drive   Mom & Dad's
building   elevator dings   third story
fridge hums through unlocked door

footsteps   whisper on carpet
guest bedroom   Mom whispers sleep
Dad   Rose   Wait   Master Suite
she reclines   on the empty bed side

he   in a place beyond sleep
wheezes   whistles   pops
upper lip shivers   nose drains
beyond three-day beard flaked

my palm   engulfs his fingers
my fingers   trace his temples
my lips   peck his forehead
my ears   pray for recognition

tell Dad   *I love you*
grasp his foot   bitter   cold
bone   Rose rubs my back
breathes *he waited for you*

## Brinksmanship

Dad
asks
*Red Sox*
*lose?* Reply
*It's football season.*
*We won The World Series in six!*
Dad chuckles *How could I forget?*
*That is won-der-ful!*
Claps hands twice.
Blows kiss.
Wipes
tear.

## April plunge

Leap into Echo Lake: ice cracks.
A twelve stroke swim through slush.
Lungs reject breath, legs thrash,
arms reach, break frozen sheets.
From a rocky ledge, cheers.
Three more strokes. Hands stutter,
knees bolt thighs to calves,
eyes seal, mouth stiffens.
Chest rams into redwood.
Shiver onto planked surface.
Wave to spectators on shore.

## Frog and toad are friends

                         I glance out the bathroom window
my young son plays with a red ball
                toss chase, toss chase
the swing-set has a fort at its base
                a fawn lies inside
        nibbles clover
my son approaches from the rear
                fawn inches out through the lattice
        steps away sniffing the lawn
my son squats where the fawn lay
           rolls his red ball

                     I rinse my razor, glance out again
my sister, on the porch of her house
            hands my son a translucent pail
            filter in the center
he scoops mud into it
           runs to a puddle
       grabs handfuls of clay
looks uphill at the stone wall

                   my son enters the bathroom
         his turn to shave
I ask him to look out the window
           can he see himself as a toddler?
I tell him this view is the apex
        of my happiness
he spies a toad leaping across the grass

## Wedding poem: we sense your love

Jenn & Adam, in this village of books and apple groves, we who love you celebrate the twining of your lives.

We sense your love online—dating profiles lead to probing questions about gastronomical experimentation. She's drawn to chicken feet, he trades them for sweetbreads. She counters *Trading feet for organ meats? glad we're talking about chickens here!*

We sense your love when he worries she'll be stranded in her apartment in a blizzard—what if the power fails? He selflessly volunteers that his wood stove generates faithful heat. Cuddle on couch, flames flare, watch snowflakes fall.

We sense your love when he's flying home from Texas, worried the blizzard will make his driveway impassable. He returns to find it clean to the blacktop—your shovel in a drift.

We sense your love reading stories to each other before bed, dream in the other's voice.

We sense your love when Blaze Dog climbs the stairs wearing the most brilliant rose, waits tail wagging to lead her to chocolates, the couple's first photo, a Valentine frame.

We sense your love in his nervousness to meet a Special Forces Dad. She's loved by both, the bond they grow is hearty and glad.

We sense your love as she laughs thinking he's cute when excited, anime cheeks, pumping fists, ignited.

We sense your love as he cares for Mema—visits, flowers, notes. She knows he'll be a doting husband, near and afar.

We sense your love when she crumbles, face in knees on the garden bed. He scoops her up, hugs to free her from fatigue.

We sense your love as she cries, startled, when he shaves his beard. He learns surprises bring her tears, never to be feared.

We know your love when he picks a tick off her hangry head while at the farm with gracious views. He pockets the engagement ring, plies her with cocoa, lunch instead—walks their warm bellies into the covered bridge, down on his knee, proposes in harmony with the lilting river.

Jenn & Adam, in this village of books and apple groves, we who love you celebrate the twining of your lives.

For Jenn & Adam with love, Pops/Dad

## The new plot

My wife and I and the dogs
fly to Sanibel Island.
            Nine days—
lovers, laughers, Gulf
beach lopers—cancer
            ignored.

My sister and brother-in-law
visit the cemetery.
            Reserve
four contiguous plots.
Easy to locate. Red rose
            bushes—

Upper row of two.
Miniature Wailing
            Wall.
Twenty feet of grass
between walkway and
            graves.

Sanibel soles crack shells.
The scan—clean enough.
            Ninety
day vacations between tests.
Heart rate of a long distance
            runner.

# Glossaries and Notes

"A wild patience has taken me this far."
~ Adrienne Rich


"One day I will find the right words, and they will be simple."
~ Jack Kerouac

## Navy Glossary for Uncle Louie poems

*Ahoy!* — call to hail a ship

*Attention on deck!* — called as soon a senior officer enters a room of junior rank personnel

blouses — Navy term for shirts

Clinometer — an instrument that measures angles of slope, elevation or depression of an object with respect to gravity

deck — floor

dog watches — a split watch, two hours for each team from 1600 to 2000

*Fair winds and following seas* — Navy blessing and farewell

garrison cap — foldable hat

Irish Pennants — loose threads

ladder — metal staircases on ships

*man the rails* — salute or render honors by standing at attention along the rails and superstructure of a ship

morning watch — 0400 to 0800

rack — bed

skivvies — underpants

*Splice the Main Brace* — give everyone their ration, bottoms-up

Springfield — M1903 Springfield, Caliber .30-06, Model 1

squared-away (shine) — perfect and in order, a boot shine that is a mirror

"Stand Navy down the field, sails set to the sky" — first line of *Anchors Aweigh*, 1906 version

swabbie — green sailor

three stripes and crow — slang for uniform insignia of Chief Petty Officers

trousers — Naval pants

*weigh anchor* — literally raising the anchor but more commonly completing all preparations for a ship to get underway

# Yiddish Glossary for Uncle Louie poems

*a shande far di kinder* — "a disgrace upon the children" shames family and future generations

beytsim — balls/testicles

boychikels, boychiks — boys

Bruder — Brother

fercockt — to be all screwed up

ganef — thief

Leybish — nickname for Louis

Mamé — Mother

Mendela — nickname for Mendel

*Nu, erst vos tut mir* — "So, what to do now"

*Oy vey* — expression of dismay

*Oy veyzmir* — stronger expression of dismay

pisher — literally a pisser, can be an insult or an endearment (it's Yiddish!)

rugelach — fruit filled pastry

schwartze — black man (from German for black), descriptive not a slur

shmendrik — a nonentity who is clueless

shtarkers — rough, tough, strong men

Shvester — Sister

Tâte — Father

tokus — buttocks, tushie

Zady — Grandfather

## Notes for Möbius Strip

I've struggled all my writing life to compose love poems. The pillars of my life are the people I love. Why is it so difficult for me to honor them?

"Möbius strip" was drafted in a Dămfino Press workshop presented by Patricia Smith. She wanted to take us to "the other side of the fence", where the demons we are unable to vanquish live. Instead, Patricia opened space for me to write a genuine love poem. Minute details are intimate, express love in the most basic ways. I've always maintained that I write the most about myself when I'm not writing about myself. Here I write most about love when not writing above love. This makes perfect sense.

As does the irony. In real life, roles reversed.

Darling, I know many of these details are personal. There is love in each. I wrote my best poem for you. Love you always from wherever.

# Notes for December 7 on the Cusp of The Millennium

"Awake ye dreamers": from this Rambam (revered Talmud annotator) quote on blowing the shofar: "Awake, ye dreamers, from your sleep, and ye drowsy ones from your lethargy; examine your deeds, repent, and remember your Creator. Ye who forget the truth in the follies of time, and spend your years in futility, look to your souls, and better your ways and actions." ~ Isaac David Essing, *The Fountain of Wisdom*.

"To punish men for their endless sins, god gave me this fair skin, this long black hair." ~ Akiko Yosano, #152 from *Tangled Hair: Selected Tanka from Midaregami*

"Tears in your eyes. You ask for sympathy. I look at the waning moon reflected on the lonely lake." ~ Akiko Yosano, #37 from *Tangled Hair: Selected Tanka from Midaregami*

"An architect proves his skill by turning the defects of a site into advantages": quote attributed to Giovanni Lorenzo Bernini, reference: R. A. Scotti, *Basilica: The Splendor and the Scandal: Building St. Peter's*

"The Bible hardly contains a command bidding us to believe...nor is any punishment assigned as awaiting him who denies it." ~ *The Dogmas of Judaism*, Solomon Schechter

tallis — prayer shawl, the fringes are cut off before dressing a body for burial

machatunim — the parents of your child's spouse

qvells — rejoices, celebrates

daven — chant prayers (rhythmically, often bowing slightly)

knaidlach — "matzah ball"

Berakhah — blessing, a prayer of thanks

## Notes for Yom Kippur D'Var Torah

D'Var Torah — teaching based on the week's Torah portion

Shema — prayer said when rising up and lying down (chanted while dying)

Kedushah — prayer blessing God's greatness

Siddur — prayer book

davens — chants prayers (rhythmically, often bowing slightly)

## Note for Committing Bill's ashes to The Gulf of Mexico...

The Mourner's Kaddish is a prayer chanted in memory of a departed person at their graveside service. The prayer continues as part of anniversary memorials (yahrzeits) and for other appropriate events.

The final verse of the prayer is:

*Oseh shalom bimrompav, hu ya'aseh shalom*
*aleinu v'al kol-yisrael, v'imru amen.*

*May the One who creates harmony on high, bring peace*
*to us and to all Israel. To which we say Amen.*

## Recommended reading

Chloé McFeters — *C is for Courage*  A coloring book of mandalas and writing journal with prompts for cancer patients and their families. Coloring allows the mind to wander. Writing has a fetching way to pull the subconscious onto the page, to reveal suppressed emotions and fears. You do not need to be a writer or artist to use this book, just a person trying to deal with cancer.
www.chloemcfeters.com/c-is-for-courage/

Dr. Paul Kalanithi — *When Breath Becomes Air*
Written by a nuerosurgeon who becomes a terminal lung cancer patient, this memoir chronicles how life changes after diagnosis. The epilogue penned by his wife broke my heart.

John Green — *The Fault in Our Stars*
This novel about two teenage cancer patients rings true. You see the cancer experience through their eyes, feel their acceptance, glimpse how enduring treatment ("bravery") becomes just another part of their lives.

For general information on cancer, start here:
www.dana-farber.org/Health-Library/

Made in the USA
Middletown, DE
26 September 2017